Deep in the Swamp

Donna M. Bateman

Illustrated by Brian Lies

SCHOLASTIC INC.

New York Toronto London Auckland Sydney
Mexico City New Delhi Hong Kong Buenos Aires

Deep in the swamp, in the warm morning sun,
Lived a mother river otter and her little pup One.
"Splash!" said the mother. "I splash," said the One.
So they splashed and they played in the warm morning sun.

Deep in the swamp, where the neverwets grew,

Lived a mother snapping turtle and her little turtles Two.

"Swim!" said the mother. "We swim," said the Two.

So they swam through the prairies where the neverwets grew.

Deep in the swamp, in a hollow cypress knee,

Lived a mother flame bird and her little chicks Three.

"Sweet-sweet!" trilled the mother. "Sweet-sweet," trilled the Three.

So they trilled loud and long in their hollow cypress knee.

Deep in the swamp, in a thicket on the shore,

Lived a mother marsh rabbit and her little bunnies Four.

"Snooze!" said the mother. "We snooze," said the Four.

So they snoozed all day long in their thicket on the shore.

Deep in the swamp, where the water lilies thrive,
Lived a mother alligator and her little gators Five.
"Bask!" said the mother. "We bask," said the Five.
So they basked in the sun where the water lilies thrive.

Deep in the swamp, in a nest built of sticks,

Lived a mother blue heron and her little chicks Six.

"Soar!" said the mother. "We soar," said the Six.

So they soared through the sky near their nest built of sticks.

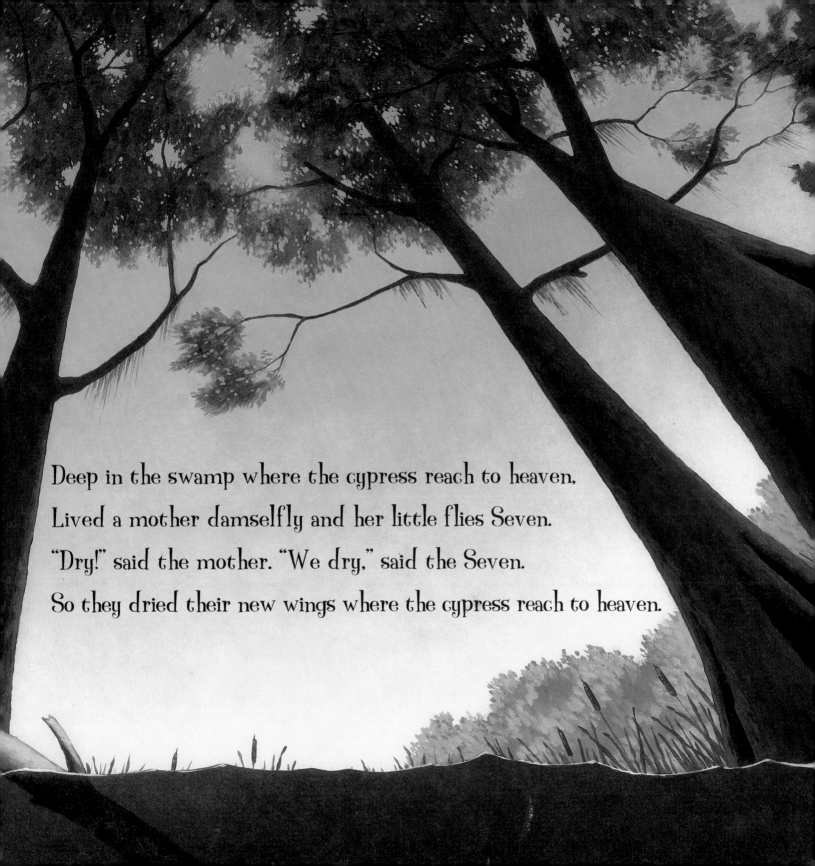

Deep in the swamp where the cypress reach to heaven,

Lived a mother damselfly and her little flies Seven.

"Dry!" said the mother. "We dry," said the Seven.

So they dried their new wings where the cypress reach to heaven.

Deep in the swamp, where the cattails grow straight,
Lived a mother bullfrog and her little froglets Eight.
"Jump!" said the mother. "We jump," said the Eight.
So they jumped through the shallows where the cattails grow straight.

Deep in the swamp, where the bamboo vines twine,
Lived a mother rat snake and her little snakes Nine.
"Climb!" said the mother. "We climb," said the Nine.
So they climbed up a pine where the bamboo vines twine.

Deep in the swamp, in an underwater den,

Lived a mother crayfish and her little crayfish Ten.

"Scurry!" said the mother. "We scurry," said the Ten.

So they scurried after tadpoles near their underwater den.

Swamp Flora and Fauna Facts

All the plants and animals in this story can be found in the Okefenokee Swamp. Many of the animals have a special relationship with their mother. However, some species do not raise their young.

alligator The largest reptiles in North America, alligators grow as long as 15 feet. Unlike most reptiles, mother alligators guard their nest and defend their babies for up to three years. Once the babies, called hatchlings, hatch, the mother leads them to water or carries them there in her mouth.

bamboo vines Bamboo vines are woody, evergreen vines with thorny stems—not to be confused with true bamboo, which is a grass. The vines grow on islands in the Okefenokee Swamp, where they tangle in the underbrush or climb trees.

blue heron The great blue heron is the largest of the herons. Great blue herons build a large nest of sticks near the top of a tree and lay three to seven eggs. Heron parents share the incubation of their eggs and the feeding of their chicks. The chicks can fly at six or seven weeks old.

bullfrog Bullfrogs are nocturnal, meaning they are active at night. They hide among plants along the water's edge. Mother bullfrogs lay up to 20,000 eggs at one time, but many of those will not live to grow into frogs. Mothers do not stay to care for the eggs or tadpoles, some of which are eaten by animals. The tadpoles, which are the larval stage of frogs, mature in one to two years.

cattails Cattails grow in lakes, ponds, marshes, ditches, and rivers. A strong stalk holds the cat's tail: a thick, velvety, brown spike that is actually the flower of the cattail plant.

crayfish

Crayfish look like small lobsters. They are mostly nocturnal and spend the day in a burrow in the mud or under rocks. Transparent, newly hatched crayfish look just like tiny adults. The babies grab onto their mother with their claws until they are ready to swim on their own.

cypress trees, cypress knees

Most of the trees in a cypress swamp are either bald cypresses or pond cypresses. All cypresses have a large trunk at the base and heavy roots that reach out to keep them standing firmly in the water. Knees often grow up from the roots and poke out of the water.

damselfly

Dameselflies have a thin, brilliantly colored body and transparent wings. They lay their eggs in the stems of water plants and then fly away. Dameselfly mothers do not raise their larvae. Dameselfly larvae look like adult dameselflies but without wings. The larvae live in the water for up to a year before climbing out and shedding their skin to complete their metamorphosis into adults.

flame bird

Prothonotary warblers are often called flame birds because of their bright golden-yellow color. Flame birds nest in a hole of a tree in or near the water and lay four to six eggs. Sometimes they nest in cypress tree knees. Only the mother bird incubates the eggs, keeping them warm with her body; but both parents feed the chicks. Although the chicks leave the nest when they are 10 or 11 days old, they are not yet good fliers.

marsh rabbit Marsh rabbits are mostly nocturnal. During the day they rest among bushes that hide them from their enemies. To escape danger, marsh rabbits run away or jump into the water, where they hide or swim to safety. Mother rabbits make their nest on the ground or in a hollow log, lining it with leaves, grass, and fur. They take care of their bunnies and nurse them for about four weeks, until they are able to feed themselves.

neverwet The true name of this yellow-tipped wetland plant is golden club. Its waxy leaves repel water, earning it the nickname "neverwet." It grows in shallow water in sunny areas of the swamp.

Okefenokee Swamp

The Okefenokee is a cypress swamp in southern Georgia and northern Florida. In addition to tall cypress trees and dim waterways, the Okefenokee Swamp also has sandy islands where pine trees grow, sunlit prairies full of water-loving plants, and clear lakes.

GEORGIA

⊙ Atlanta

Okefenokee Swamp

FLORIDA

prairie   In the Okefenokee Swamp, prairies are open marshes covered with shallow water and filled with water-loving plants such as neverwets, water lilies, grasses, ferns, rushes, reeds, and cattails.

rat snake   Rat snakes can grow as long as seven feet. They can climb trees and swim. Yellow rat snakes are nocturnal in the summer but are active during the day the rest of the year. They hide their eggs under rocks, hollow logs, or leaves or in abandoned burrows. Mothers sometimes coil around their eggs but do not raise their babies.

river otter

River otters are excellent swimmers and can swim a long way underwater before coming up for air. They are fun-loving mammals that like to splash, wrestle, and play tag. Mother otters nest in abandoned burrows beside streams or lakes. The mothers care for the pups alone for several months, but the father otter may help later.

snapping turtle

Snapping turtles cannot pull their legs and head completely into their shell to hide. Instead, they bite their enemies. During the day, snappers rest in muddy areas or shallow waters. They hunt mostly at night. With only their eyes and nostrils poking out of the water, snappers wait for prey to swim by them. Mother snapping turtles lay their eggs in a nest hole and then leave. They don't protect the nest or raise the babies that hatch. The hatchlings hide until they are ready to make their way to water.

swamp In a swamp, shallow water covers almost all the land. Trees, bushes, and other plants grow in the water.

water lilies The blossoms and leaves, or pads, of water lilies float on the water; the stem reaches down and is rooted in the mud. Frogs, turtles, and insects may rest on the lily pads. Some animals even use the pads as a bridge to walk across the water.

For Eric and Paige, the two little ones in my house, and especially for Brian (with many thanks to Randi)—D. M. B.

To my mother, who raised writers Two—B. L.

ISBN-13: 978-0-545-06695-2
ISBN-10: 0-545-06695-6

Text copyright © 2007 by Donna M. Bateman.
Illustrations copyright © 2007 by Brian Lies. All rights reserved. Published by Scholastic Inc., 557 Broadway, New York, NY 10012, by arrangement with Charlesbridge Publishing. SCHOLASTIC and associated logos are trademarks and/or registered trademarks of Scholastic Inc.

12   14 15 16/0

Printed in the U.S.A.   40

First Scholastic printing, April 2008

Illustrations done in acrylics on Strathmore paper
Display type and text type set in Pink Martini, designed by Jess Latham of Blue Vinyl Fonts, Falkville, AL
Designed by Susan Mallory Sherman